SPIRITUAL SONGS

COLOSSIANS III. 16.

Being One Hundred Hymns

NOT TO BE FOUND IN THE HYMN BOOKS COMMONLY USED.

SELECTED BY THE

REV. J. C. RYLE, B.A.,

RECTOR OF HELMINGHAM, SUFFOLK.

NEW AMERICAN, FROM THE ENLARGED ENGLISH EDITION.

NEW-YORK:

ANSON D. F. RANDOLPH, 770 BROADWAY,

CORNER OF NINTH STREET.

1868.

Sing ye praises with understanding

(Psalm xlvii. 7.)

SPIRITUAL SONGS.

1. *Coloss.* i. 19. **7, 6.**

1 I lay my sins on Jesus,
The spotless Lamb of God;
He bears them all, and frees us
From the accursed load.
I bring my guilt to Jesus,
To wash my crimson stains
White, in his blood most precious,
Till not a spot remains.

2 I lay my wants on Jesus;
All fullness dwells in Him;
He heals all my diseases,
He doth my soul redeem.
I lay my griefs on Jesus,
My burdens and my cares;
He from them all releases,
He all my sorrow shares.

3 I rest my soul on Jesus,
  This weary soul of mine;
His right hand me embraces,
  I on His breast recline.
I love the name of Jesus,
  Immanuel, Christ, the Lord;
Like fragrance on the breezes
  His name abroad is poured.

4 I long to be like Jesus,
  Meek, loving, lowly, mild;
I long to be like Jesus,
  The Father's holy child.
I long to be with Jesus,
  Amid the heavenly throng,
To sing with saints His praises,
  To learn the angels' song.

H. BONAR.

2. *Matt.* vi. 12. 7's

1 When this passing world is done,
When has sunk yon glaring sun,
When we stand with Christ in glory,
Looking o'er life's finished story,
Then, Lord, shall I fully know—
Not till then—how much I owe.

2 When I hear the wicked call
On the rocks and hills to fall;
When I see them start and shrink
On the fiery deluge brink,
Then, Lord, shall I fully know—
Not till then—how much I owe.

3 When I stand before the throne,
Dressed in beauty not my own,
When I see Thee as Thou art,
Love thee with unsinning heart,
Then, Lord, shall I fully know—
Not till then—how much I owe.

4 When the praise of heaven I hear,
Loud as thunders to the ear,
Loud as many waters' noise,
Sweet as harp's melodious voice,
Then, Lord, shall I fully know—
Not till then—how much I owe.

5 Chosen not for good in me,
Wakened up from wrath to flee,
Hidden in the Saviour's side,
By the Spirit sanctified;
Teach me, Lord, on earth to show,
By my love, how much I owe.

6 Oft I walk beneath the cloud,
Dark as midnight's gloomy shroud;
But when fear is at the height,
Jesus comes, and all is light.
Blessed Jesus! bid me show
Doubting saints how much I owe.

R. M. M'CHEYNE.

3. 1 *Peter* v. 7. C.M.

1 Lord, it belongs not to my care,
Whether I die or live;
To love and serve Thee is my share,
And this Thy grace must give.

2 If life be long, I will be glad,
That I may long obey;
If short, yet why should I be sad
To soar to endless day?

3 Christ leads me through no darker rooms
Than He went through before;
He that unto God's kingdom comes,
Must enter by His door.

4 Come, Lord, when grace has made me
Thy blessed face to see; [meet,
For if thy work on earth be sweet,
What will thy glory be?

5 Then shall I end my sad complaints,
And weary sinful days,
And join with the triumphant saints
That sing Jehovah's praise.

6 My knowledge of that life is small,
The eye of faith is dim;
But 'tis enough that Christ knows all,
And I shall be with Him.

R. BAXTER.

4.* *John* vi. 37. **P.M.**

1 Just as I am, without one plea,
But that thy blood was shed for me,
And that thou bid'st me come to Thee,
O Lamb of God, I come!

* The metre of this most beautiful hymn is one with which few are acquainted. It may, however, be sung to a long-measure tune, by repeating the words, "I come," in the fourth line of each verse. It will be found arranged for music in Mr. Lowell Mason's work, *The Hallelujah*.

2 Just as I am, and waiting not
To rid my soul of one dark blot, [spot,
To Thee, whose blood can cleanse each
O Lamb of God, I come!

3 Just as I am, though tossed about
With many a conflict, many a doubt,
With fears within and wars without,
O Lamb of God, I come!

4 Just as I am, poor, wretched, blind,
Sight, riches, healing of the mind,
Yea, all I need, in Thee to find,
O Lamb of God, I come!

5 Just as I am—Thou wilt receive,
Wilt welcome, pardon, cleanse, relieve,
Because thy promise I believe—
O Lamb of God, I come!

6 Just as I am—Thy love unknown
Has broken every barrier down;
Now to be Thine, yea, thine alone—
O Lamb of God, I come!

5. *Isaiah* xxvi. 4. **S.M.**

1 Give to the winds thy fears,
Hope, and be undismayed;
God hears thy sighs, and counts thy tears,
God shall lift up thy head.

2 Through waves, and clouds, and storms,
He gently clears the way:
Wait thou His time; so shall this night
Soon end in joyous day.

3 Still heavy is thy heart?
Still sink thy spirits down?
Cast off the weight, let fear depart,
And every care be gone.

4 What though thou rulest not?
Yet heaven, and earth, and hell
Proclaim God sitteth on the throne,
And ruleth all things well.

5 Leave to His sovereign sway,
To choose and to command;
So shalt thou, wondering, own His way
How wise, how good His hand!

6 Far, far above thy thought,
His counsel shall appear,
When fully He the work hath wrought,
That caused thy needless fear.

6. *Psalm* xxxi. 15. S.M.

1 Our times are in Thy hand,
O God, we wish them there;
Our life, our friends, our souls we leave
Entirely to Thy care.

2 Our times are in Thy hand,
Whatever they may be,
Pleasing or painful, dark or bright,
As best may seem to Thee.

3 Our times are in Thy hand,
Why should we doubt or fear?
A Father's hand will never cause
His child a needless tear.

4 Our times are in Thy hand,
Jesus the crucified;
The hand our many sins have pierced,
Is now our guard and guide.

Our times are in Thy hand,
We'll always trust in Thee,
Till we have left this weary land,
And all Thy glory see.

7. *Heb.* xii. 2. 7's.

1 When along life's thorny road,
Faints the soul beneath the load,
By its cares and sins opprest,
Finds on earth no peace or rest:
When the wily tempter's near,
Filling us with doubts and fear,
Jesus, to Thy feet we flee,
Jesus, we will look to Thee.

2 Thou, our Saviour, from the throne,
List'nest to Thy people's moan;
Thou, the living Head, dost share
Every pang thy members bear.
Full of tenderness Thou art;
Thou wilt heal the broken heart;
Full of power, Thine arm shall quell
All the rage and might of hell!

3 By Thy tears o'er Lazarus shed,
By Thy power to raise the dead,
By Thy meekness under scorn,
By Thy stripes and crown of thorn,

By that rich and precious blood,
That hath made our peace with God
Jesus, to Thy feet we flee;
Jesus, we will cling to Thee.

4 Mighty to redeem and save,
Thou hast overcome the grave;
Thou the bars of death hast riven,
Opened wide the gates of heaven;
Soon in glory Thou shalt come,
Taking Thy poor pilgrims home;
Jesus, then we all shall be,
Ever—ever—Lord, with Thee.

8. 1 *Thess.* iv. 17. S.M.

1 For ever with the Lord!
Amen, so let it be:
Life from the dead is in that word,
'Tis immortality.

2 Here in the body pent,
Absent from Him I roam,
Yet nightly pitch my moving tent
A day's march nearer home.

3 My Father's house on high,
Home of my soul, how near
At times to Faith's illumined eye
Thy golden gates appear!

4 My thirsty spirit faints
To reach the land I love,
The bright inheritance of saints,
Jerusalem above.

5 Yet clouds will intervene,
And all my prospect flies;
Like Noah's dove, I flit between
Rough seas and stormy skies.

6 Anon the clouds depart,
The winds and waters cease,
While sweetly o'er my gladdened heart
Expands the bow of peace.

9. *Rom.* viii. 1. C.M.

1 No condemnation! O my soul,
'Tis God that speaks the word;
Perfect in comeliness art thou,
In Christ thy glorious Lord.

2 In heaven His blood for ever speaks,
In God the Father's ear;
His church, the jewels, on his heart,
Jesus will ever bear.

3 No condemnation! precious word!
Consider it, my soul;
Thy sins were all on Jesus laid;
His stripes have made thee whole.

4 Teach us, O God, to fix our eyes
On Christ, the spotless Lamb,
So shall we love Thy gracious will,
And glorify Thy name

10. 2 *Cor.* v. 14, 15. **7, 6.**

1 O Lord, who now art seated
Above the heavens on high,
(The gracious work completed,
For which Thou cam'st to die,)
To Thee our hearts are lifted,
While pilgrims wandering here,
For Thou alone art gifted,
Our every weight to bear.

2 We know that Thou hast bought us,
And washed us in Thy blood;
We know Thy grace has brought us,
As kings and priests to God.
We know that soon the morning,
Long looked for, hasteth near,
When we, at Thy returning,
In glory shall appear.

3 O Lord, Thy love's unbounded!
So full, so sweet, so free!
Our thoughts are all confounded,
Whene'er we think on Thee:
For us Thou cam'st from heaven,
For us to bleed and die;
That purchased and forgiven,
We might ascend on high.

4 Oh! let this love constrain us
To give our hearts to Thee;
Let nothing henceforth pain us,
But that which paineth Thee.
Our joy, our one endeavor,
Through suffering, conflict, shame—
To serve Thee, gracious Saviour,
And magnify Thy name.

11. *Isaiah* iii. 10. S.M.

1 What cheering words are these;
Their sweetness who can tell?
In time and to eternal days,
"'Tis with the righteous well."

2 In every state secure,
Kept as Jehovah's eye,
'Tis well with them while life endures,
And well when called to die.

3 Well when they see His face,
Or sink amidst the flood;
Well in affliction's thorny maze,
Or on the mount with God.

4 'Tis well when joys arise,
'Tis well when sorrows flow,
'Tis well when darkness veils the skies
And strong temptations grow.

5 'Tis well when Jesus calls,
"From earth and sin arise,
To join the hosts of ransomed souls,
Made to salvation wise."

12. *Matt.* xiv. 28, 29. P M

1 He bids us come; His voice we know,
And boldly on the waters go,
To Him our Lord and God;
We walk on life's tempestuous sea,
For He who died to set us free,
Hath called us by His word.

2 Secure from troubled waves we tread,
Nor all the storms around us heed,
While to our Lord we look;

O'er every fierce temptation bound,
The billows yield a solid ground,
The wave is firm as rock.

3 But if from Him we turn our eye,
And see the raging floods run high,
And feel our fears within;
Our foes so strong, our flesh so frail,
Reason and unbelief prevail,
And sink us into sin.

4 Lord, we our belief confess,
Our little spark of faith increase,
That we may doubt no more;
But fix on Thee our steady eye,
And on Thine outstretched arm rely,
Till all the storm is o'er.

13. *Galat.* vi. 9. 7's

1 Faint not, Christian! though the road
Leading to thy blest abode,
Darksome be, and dangerous too—
Christ, thy guide, will bring thee through.

2 Faint not, Christian! though in rage,
Satan would thy soul engage;
Gird on faith's anointed shield,
Bear it to the battle-field.

3 Faint not, Christian! though the world,
Has its hostile flag unfurled;
Hold the cross of Jesus fast,
Thou shalt overcome at last.

4 Faint not, Christian! though within,
There's a heart so prone to sin;
Christ the Lord is over all,
He'll not suffer thee to fall.

5 Faint not, Christian! though thy God
Smite thee with His chastening rod;
Smite He must, with father's care,
That He may His love declare.

6 Faint not, Christian! Jesus' near,
Soon in glory He'll appear;
And His love will then bestow
Power over every foe.

7 Faint not, Christian! look on high,
See the harpers in the sky;
Patient wait, and thou wilt join—
Chant with them of love divine.

14. *Prov.* xviii. 10. L.M.

1 Rejoice ye saints, rejoice and praise
The blessings of redeeming grace;
Jesus, your everlasting tower,
Mocks at the angry tempest's power.

2 His love's a refuge ever nigh,
His watchfulness as mountains high,
His name's a rock, which winds above,
And waves below, can never move.

3 While all things change, He changes not,
He ne'er forgets, though oft forgot;
His love's unchangeably the same,
And as enduring as His name.

4 Rejoice, ye saints, rejoice and praise
The blessings of this wondrous grace;
Jesus, your everlasting tower,
Can bear unmoved the tempest's power.

15. *John* xiv. 1, 2. P.M.

1 Away with our sorrow and fear!
We soon shall have entered our home;
The city of saints shall appear,
The day of eternity come.

From earth we shall quickly remove,
  To dwell in a native abode,
In mansions of glory above,
  Prepared of our Father and God.

2 Ah! who upon earth can conceive
  The bliss that in heaven they'll share,
And who this dark world would not leave
  And cheerfully seek to be there,
Where Christ is the light and the sun,
  And we by reflection shall shine,
With Him everlastingly one,
  And bright in effulgence divine.

3 'Tis good at Thy word to be here,
  'Tis better in Thee to be gone,
And see Thee in glory appear,
  And rise to a share in Thy throne.
All tears will be wiped from our eyes,
  When Thee we behold in the cloud,
And echo the joys of the skies,
  And shout to the trumpet of God.

16. 1 *Cor.* xv. 10. C.M.

1 All that I *was*, my sin, my guilt,
  My death, was all my own;
All that I *am*, I owe to Thee,
  My gracious God alone.

2 The evil of my former state
  Was mine, and only mine;
The good in which I now rejoice
  Is Thine, and only Thine.

3 The darkness of my former state,
  The bondage, all was mine;
The light of life in which I walk,
  The liberty is Thine.

4 Thy grace first made me feel my sin,
  And taught me to believe;
Then in believing, peace I found,
  And now I live, I live.

5 All that I am e'en here on earth,
  All that I hope to be,
When Jesus comes, and glory dawns,
  I owe it, Lord, to Thee.

H. BONAR.

17. 1 *Peter* ii. 7. **C.M.**

1 We'll sing of Christ, no matter who
  Should disapprove the theme:
When He is precious to our view,
  We can't but sing of Him.

2 And He is precious in the sight
Of all who know His voice:
'Twas He who brought them to the light,
And taught them to rejoice.

3 'Tis He who cheers them by His smile,
And guards them by His power;
Who keeps them safe from force and guile,
In every trying hour.

4 'Tis He who will conduct them home,
Beyond the reach of ill:
Where all the ransomed people come,
Where saints for ever dwell.

5 Then let His people make their boast
Of Him and Him alone,
Who came from heaven to save the lost;
The praise be His alone.

18. *Exodus* xiv. 15. 7's.

1 When we cannot see our way,
Let us trust, and still obey;
He who bids us forward go,
Cannot fail the way to show.

2 Though the sea be deep and wide,
Though a passage seem denied;
Fearless let us still proceed,
Since the Lord vouchsafes to lead.

3 Though it seems the gloom of night,
Though we see no ray of light;
Since the Lord Himself is there,
'Tis not meet that we should fear.

4 Night with Him is never night,
Where He is, there all is light;
When He calls us, why delay?
They are happy who obey.

5 Be it ours, then, while we're here,
Him to follow without fear!
Where He calls us, there to go,
What He bids us, that to do.

19. *Heb.* x. 37. L.M.

1 "A little while," our Lord shall come,
And we shall wander here no more;
He'll take us to our Father's home,
Where He for us has gone before.

2 "A little while," He'll come again;
Let us the precious hours redeem;
Our only grief to give Him pain,
Our joy to serve and follow Him.

3 "A little while," 'twill soon be past;
Why should we shun the promised cross?
Oh! let us in His footsteps haste,
Counting for Him all else but loss.

4 "A little while," come, Saviour, come;
For Thee Thy bride has tarried long;
Take Thy poor wearied pilgrims home,
To sing the new eternal song.

20. *Matt.* xviii. 20. 8, 7, 4.

1 In Thy name, O Lord, assembling,
We, Thy people, now draw near;
Teach us to rejoice with trembling;
Speak and let Thy servants hear,
Hear with meekness.
Hear Thy word with godly fear.

2 While our days on earth are lengthened,
May we give them, Lord, to Thee,
Cheered by hope, and daily strengthened,
May we run, nor weary be;
'Till Thy glory,
Without clouds in heaven we see.

3 Then in worship, purer, sweeter,
Thee Thy people shall adore,
Tasting of enjoyment greater
Far than thought conceived before.
Full enjoyment,
Full, unmixed, and evermore.

21. 2 *Peter* iii. 12. **P.M**

1 Oh! haste away, my brethren dear,
And come to Canaan's shore;
We'll meet and sing for ever there,
When all our toils are o'er.

Oh! that will be joyful, joyful, joyful,
Oh! that will be joyful,
To meet to part no more,
To meet to part no more,
On Canaan's happy shore;
And there sing hallelujah
With the friends that have gone before.

2 How sweet to hear the hallowed theme
That saints shall ever sing;
To hear their voices all proclaim
"Salvation to the King."

Oh! that will be, etc.

3 Around His throne, all clothed in white,
Will all His saints appear;
And, shining in His glory bright,
Will see our Saviour there.

Oh! that will be, etc.

4 Through heaven the shouts of angels ring
When sons to God are born:
Oh! what a company will sing
On the millennial morn.

Oh! that will be, etc.

5 Through one eternal day we'll sing,
And bless His sacred name,
With hallelujah to the King,
And 'Worthy is the Lamb."

Oh! that will be, etc.

22. *Rom.* xxii. 20. P.M.

1 The church has waited long
Her absent Lord to see;
And still in loneliness she waits—
A friendless stranger she.

Age after age has gone,
  Sun after sun has set,
And still in weeds of widowhood
  She weeps, a mourner yet.

Come, then, Lord Jesus, come!

2 Saint after saint on earth,
  Has lived, and loved, and died;
And as they left us, one by one,
  We laid them side by side:
We laid them down to sleep,
  But not in hope forlorn;
We laid them but to ripen there
  Till the last glorious morn.

Come, then, Lord Jesus, come!

3 The serpent's brood increase,
  The powers of hell grow bold,
The conflict thickens, faith is low,
  And love is waxing cold.
How long, O Lord our God,
  Holy, and true, and good,
Wilt thou not judge Thy suffering church,
  Her sighs, and tears, and blood?

Come, then, Lord Jesus, come!

4 We long to hear Thy voice,
  To see Thee face to face,
To share Thy crown and glory then,
  As now we share Thy grace.
Should not the loving bride
  The absent bridegroom mourn?
Should she not wear the weeds of grief
  Until her Lord return?

Come, then, Lord Jesus, come!

5 The whole creation groans,
  And waits to hear that voice
That shall restore her comeliness,
  And make her wastes rejoice.
Come, Lord, and wipe away
  The curse, the sin, the stain,
And make this blighted world of ours
  Thine own fair world again.

Come, then, Lord Jesus, come!

H. BONAR.

23. *Cant.* viii. 5. P.M.

1 O holy Saviour! Friend unseen!
Since on thy arm thou bid'st us lean,
Help us throughout life's changing scene
  By faith to cling to Thee.

2 Blest with this fellowship divine,
Take what Thou wilt, we'll not repine
For, as the branches to the vine,
We only cling to Thee.

3 Though far from home, fatigued, opprest,
Here we have found a place of rest;
As exiles still, yet not unblest,
Because we cling to Thee.

4 What though the world deceitful prove,
And earthly friends and hopes remove.
With patient, uncomplaining love,
Still can we cling to Thee.

5 Though oft we seem to tread alone
Life's dreary waste with thorns o'ergrown,
Thy voice of love, in gentlest tone,
Whispers, "Still cling to Me!"

6 Though faith and hope are often tried,
We ask not, need not, aught beside,
So safe, so calm, so satisfied
The souls that cling to Thee.

7 They fear not Satan, nor the grave,
They know Thee near, and strong to save
With Thee all danger they can brave,
Because thy cling to Thee.

8 Blest is our lot, whate'er befall;
Who can affright, or who appal;
Since as our strength, our Rock, our all,
Jesus, we cling to Thee?

24. *Galat.* vi. 14. C.M

1 Let worldly minds the world pursue;
What are its charms to me?
Once I admired its trifles too,
But grace has set me free.

2 Its pleasures now no longer please,
No more content afford;
Far from my heart be joys like these,
Now I have seen the Lord.

3 As by the light of opening day
The stars are all concealed,
So earthly pleasures fade away
When Jesus is revealed.

4 Creatures no more divide my choice,
I bid you all depart;
His name, and love, and gracious word,
Have fixed my roving heart.

25. *Galat.* iii. 13. C.M.

1 Blessed be God, for ever blest,
And glorious be His name!
His Son He gave, our souls to save
From everlasting shame.

2 Had I worn sackcloth, and in dust
Cast myself humbly down,
Covered my miserable head
With ashes for a crown,

3 This could not save me from the curse,
Nor end the endless pain,
Nor quench the fire, nor ease the heart,
Nor wipe away one stain.

4 Th' Eternal Life His life laid down,
Such was the wondrous plan,
And God, the blessed God, was made
A curse for cursed man.

5 Our flesh He took, our sins He bore,
Himself for us He gave;
His woes were ours, and we with Him
Were buried in one grave.

6 With Him we rose, with Him we live
With Him we sit above,
With Him for ever we shall share
The Father's boundless love.

7 Bless, then, Jehovah's blessed name,
And bless our blessed King;
And songs of glad deliverance
For ever, ever sing!

26. *Matt.* xi. 28. Double C.M.

1 I heard the voice of Jesus say,
Come unto me and rest;
Lay down, thou weary one, lay down
Thy head upon my breast.
I came to Jesus as I was,
Weary, and worn, and sad,
I found in Him a resting-place,
And He has made me glad.

2 I heard the voice of Jesus say,
Behold, I freely give
The living water; thirsty one,
Stoop down and drink and live.
I came to Jesus, and I drank
Of that life-giving stream;
My thirst was quenched, my soul revived,
And now I live in Him.

3 I heard the voice of Jesus say,
I am this dark world's light,
Look unto me, thy morn shall rise,
And all thy day be bright.
I looked to Jesus, and I found
In Him my Star, my Sun;
And in that light of life I'll walk,
Till travelling days are done.

H. BONAR.

27. *Ephes.* v. 30. C.M.

1 Lord Jesus, are we one with Thee?
Oh! height, oh! depth of love!
With Thee we died upon the tree,
In Thee we live above.

2 Such was Thy grace that for our sake
Thou didst from heaven come down,
Our mortal flesh and blood partake,
In all our misery one.

3 Our sins, our guilt, in love divine,
Were borne on earth by Thee;
The gall, the curse, the wrath were Thine,
To set Thy members free.

4 Ascended now in glory bright,
Still one with us Thou art;
Nor life, nor death, nor depth, nor height
Thy saints and Thee can part.

5 Soon, soon shall come that glorious day
When, seated on Thy throne,
Thou shalt to wond'ring worlds display
That Thou with us art one.

28. *Prov.* xiv. 32. 7 6.

1 Ah! I shall soon be dying,
Time swiftly glides away;
But, on my Lord relying,
I hail the happy day;
The day when I shall enter
Upon a world unknown.
My helpless soul I venture
On Jesus Christ alone.

2 He once, a spotless victim,
Upon Mount Calvary bled;
Jehovah did afflict Him
And bruise Him in my stead:
Hence all my hope arises,
Unworthy as I am;
My soul most surely prizes
The sin-atoning Lamb.

3 Soon, with the saints in glory,
The grateful song I'll raise,
And chant my blissful story
In high seraphic lays.
Free grace, redeeming merit,
And sanctifying love
Of Father, Son, and Spirit,
I'll sing in realms above.

29. *Philip.* i. 21. P.M.

1 Rejoice for a brother deceased,
Our loss is his infinite gain;
A soul out of prison released,
And freed from its bodily chain.
With songs let us follow his flight,
And mount with his spirit above,
Escaped to the mansions of light,
And lodged in the Eden of love.

2 Our brother the haven hath gained,
    Out-flying the tempest and wind;
  His rest he hath sooner obtained,
    And left his companions behind,
  Still tossed on a sea of distress,
    Hard toiling to make the blest shore,
  Where all is assurance and peace,
    And sorrow and sin are no more.

3 There all the ship's company meet,
    Who sailed with the Saviour beneath,
  With shouting each other they greet,
    And triumph o'er trouble and death.
  The voyage of life's at an end,
    The mortal affliction is past;
  The age that in heaven they spend
    For ever and ever shall last.

C. WESLEY.

30. *Rev.* xiv. 13. **P.M.**

1 How blest is our sister, bereft
    Of all that could burden her mind!
  How easy the soul that has left.
    This wearisome body behind;
  Of evil incapable thou
    Whose relics with envy I see;
  No longer in misery now,
    No longer a sinner like me.

2 This earth is affected no more
 With sickness, or shaken with pain:
The war in the members is o'er,
 And never shall vex her again.
No anger henceforward, or shame,
 Shall redden this innocent clay;
Extinct is the animal flame,
 And passion is vanquished away.

3 This languishing head is at rest,
 Its thinking and aching are o'er;
This quiet, immovable breast
 Is heaved by affliction no more;
This heart is no longer the seat
 Of trouble and torturing pain;
It ceases to flutter and beat,
 It never shall flutter again.

4 The lids she so seldom could close,
 By sorrow forbidden to sleep,
Sealed up in their mortal repose,
 Have strangely forgotten to weep:
The fountains can yield no supplies,
 These hollows from water are free;
The tears are all wiped from these eyes,
 And evil they never shall see.

C. WESLEY.

31. *Rom.* viii. 31. **7, 6**

1 Is God for me? what is it
  That man can do to me?
Oft as my God I visit,
  All woes give way and flee.
If God be my salvation,
  My refuge in distress,
What earthly tribulation
  Can shake my steadfast peace?

2 The ground of my profession
  Is Jesus and His blood;
He gives me the possession
  Of everlasting good.
In me, and in my doing,
  Is nothing on this earth;
What Jesus is bestowing
  Alone is truly worth.

3 For me there is provided
  A city fair and new;
To it I shall be guided—
  Jerusalem the true!
My portion there is lying,
  A destined Canaan—lot;
Though I am daily dying,
  My Canaan withers not.

4 My heart within me leapeth,
And cannot down be cast;
In sunshine bright it keepeth,
A never-ending feast.
The sun which, smiling, lights me
Is Jesus Christ alone;
And what to sing invites me,
Is heaven on earth begun.

32. 2 *Kings* iv. 26. P.M.

1 Through the love of God our Saviour,
All will be well;
Free and changeless is His favour,
All, all is well.
Precious is the blood that healed us;
Perfect is the grace that sealed us,
Strong the hand stretched out to shield us,
All must be well.

2 Though we pass through tribulation,
All will be well;
Our's is such a full salvation,
All, all is well.
Happy, still to God confiding,
Fruitful, if in Christ abiding,
Holy, through the Spirit's guiding,
All must be well.

3 We expect a bright to-morrow,
      All will be well;
   Faith can sing through days of sorrow
      All, all is well.
   On our Father's love relying,
   Jesus every need supplying,
   Or in living or in dying,
      All must be well.

33. *Matt.* xiv. 27. C.M.

1 When waves of sorrow round me swell,
      My soul is not dismayed;
   I hear a voice I know full well,
      "'Tis I, be not afraid."

2 When black the threat'ning clouds appear
      And storms my path invade,
   That voice shall tranquilize each fear,
      "'Tis I, be not afraid."

3 There is a gulf that must be crossed,—
      Saviour! be near to aid;
   Whisper, when my frail bark is tossed,
      "'Tis I, be not afraid."

4 There is a dark and fearful vale,
Death hides within its shade;
Oh! say, when flesh and hearts shall fail,
"'Tis I, be not afraid."

34. *John* xvii. 24. L.M.

1 Let me be with Thee where Thou art,
My Saviour, my eternal rest;
Then only will this longing heart
Be fully and for ever blest.

2 Let me be with Thee where Thou art,
Thy unveiled glory to behold;
Then only will this wand'ring heart
Cease to be false to Thee, and cold.

3 Let me be with Thee where Thou art,
Where spotless saints Thy name adore;
Then only will this sinful heart
Be evil and defiled no more.

4 Let me be with Thee where Thou art,
Where none can die, where none remove,
There neither death nor life will part
Me from Thy presence and Thy love.

35. *Matt.* vi. 10. P.M.

1 My God, my Father, while I stray,
Far from my home, on life's rough way,
Oh! teach me from my heart to say,
"Thy will be done."

2 If Thou should'st call me to resign
What most I prize,—it ne'er was mine;
I only yield Thee what was Thine;—
"Thy will be done."

3 E'en if again I ne'er should see
The friend more dear than life to me,
Ere long we both shall be with Thee;-
"Thy will be done."

4 Should pining sickness waste away
My life in premature decay,
My Father, still I strive to say,
"Thy will be done."

5 If but my fainting heart be blest
With Thy sweet Spirit for its guest,
My God, to Thee I leave the rest,—
"Thy will be done."

6 Renew my wil. from day to day,
Blend it with Thine, and take away
All that now makes it hard to say,
"Thy will be done."

7 Then when on earth I breathe no more,
The prayer oft mixed with tears before,
I'll sing upon a happier shore,
"Thy will be done."

36. *Rom.* viii. 28. C M.

1 When I by faith the Saviour's death
Behold, and know Him mine,
Sweetly my rising hours advance,
And peacefully decline.

2 I can not doubt his bounteous love,
So full, so free, so kind;
To His unerring, gracious will
Be ev'ry wish resigned.

3 Good when he gives, supremely good,
Nor less when he denies;
Afflictions from His gracious hand,
Are blessings in disguise.

4 Inscribed in Thy fair book of life,
Oh! may I read my name!
There let it fill some humble place,
Beneath the slaughtered Lamb!

37. *Rev.* v. 12. **P.M**

1 Glory to God on high!
Let heav'n and earth reply,
Praise ye His name:
His love and grace adore,
Who all our sorrows bore;
Sing aloud evermore,
"Worthy the Lamb!"

2 Jesus, our Lord and God,
Bore sin's tremendous load;
Praise ye His name:
Tell what His arm hath done,
What spoils from death He won;
Sing His great name alone;
"Worthy the Lamb!"

3 Join, all ye ransomed race,
Our Lord and God to bless;
Praise ye His name;

In him we will rejoice,
And make a cheerful noise,
Shouting with heart and voice,
"Worthy the Lamb!"

4 What though we change our place,
Yet we shall never cease
Praising His name:
To Him our songs we bring,
Hail Him our gracious King,
And without ceasing sing,
"Worthy the Lamb!"

5 Let all the hosts above
Join in one song of love,
Praising His name:
To Him ascribed be,
Honour and majesty,
Through all eternity:
"Worthy the Lamb!"

38. *Psalm* cxxxiv. 1. S.M.

1 Stand up and bless the Lord,
Ye people of His choice;
Stand up and bless the Lord your God,
With heart and soul and voice.

2 Though high above all praise,
  Above all blessing high,
Who would not fear His holy name,
  And laud and magnify?

3 Oh! for the living flame,
  From His own altar brought,
To touch our lips, our minds inspire,
  And wing to heaven our thought!

4 God is our strength and song,
  And His salvation ours;
Then be His love in Christ proclaimed,
  With all our ransomed powers.

5 Stand up and bless the Lord,
  The Lord your God adore;
Stand up and bless His glorious name,
  Henceforth for evermore.

MONTGOMERY.

39. *Luke* xxi. 28. C.M.

1 Awake ye saints, and raise your eyes,
  And lift your voices high;
Extol the sovereign love that shews
  Our full redemption nigh.

2 Fast on the wings of time it flies,
Its coming nought can stay:
It speeds with each revolving year,
With each declining day.

3 Not many years their rounds shall run,
Nor many mornings rise,
Ere all its glories stand revealed
To our admiring eyes.

4 Then let the wheels of nature roll
Yet onward to decay:
We long to hail the rising sun,
That brings th' eternal day.

DODDRIDGE.

40. 1 *John* iv. 19. Double C.M.

1 We love Thee, Lord, because when we
Had erred and gone astray,
Thou didst recall our wand'ring souls
Into the homeward way.
When helpless, hopeless, we were lost
In sin and sorrow's night,
Thou did'st send forth a guiding ray
Of Thy benignant light.

2 Because when we forsook Thy ways,
Nor kept Thy holy will,
Thou wert not an avenging Judge,
But a gracious Father still.
Because we have forgot Thee, Lord,
But Thou hast not forgot,—
Because we have forsaken Thee,
But Thou forsakest not.

3 Because, O Lord, Thou lovedst us
With everlasting love;
Because Thou gav'st Thy Son to die,
That we might live above;
Because when we were heirs of wrath,
Thou gav'st the hopes of heaven;
We love because we much have sinned,
And much have been forgiven.

41. 1 *John* ii. 1. P.M.

1 O Thou, the contrite sinner's Friend!
Who loving, lov'st them to the end,
On this alone my hopes depend,
That Thou wilt plead for me.

2 When weary in the Christian race,
Far off appears my resting place,
And, fainting, I mistrust Thy grace,
Then, Saviour, plead for me.

3 When I have erred and gone astray,
Afar from thine and wisdom's way,
And see no glimm'ring, guiding ray,
Still, Saviour, plead for me.

4 When Satan, by my sins made bold,
Strives from Thy cross to loose my hold,
Then with Thy pitying arms enfold,
And plead, oh! plead for me.

5 And when my dying hour draws near,
Darkened with anguish, guilt, and fear,
Then to my fainting sight appear,
Pleading in heaven for me.

6 When the full light of heavenly day,
Reveals my sin in dread array,
Say Thou hast washed them all away,—
Oh! say Thou plead'st for me!

WESLEY.

42. *Rom.* v. 1. P.M.

1 I thought upon my sins, and I was sad,
My soul was troubled sore and filled with pain;
But then I thought on Jesus and was glad,
My heavy grief was turned tc joy again.

2 I thought upon the law, the fiery law,
Holy, and just, and good in its decree,
I looked to Jesus, and in Him I saw
That law fulfilled, its curse endured for me.

3 I thought I saw an angry, frowning God,
Sitting as judge upon the great white throne;
My soul was overwhelmed,—then Jesus shewed
His gracious face, and all my dread was gone.

4 I saw my sad estate, condemned to die;
Then terror seized my heart and dark despair;
But when to Calvary I turned my eye,
I saw the cross, and read forgiveness there.

5 I saw that I was lost, far gone astray,
No hope of safe return, there seemed to be;
But then I heard that Jesus was the way,
A new and living way prepared for me.

6 Then in that way, so free, so safe, so sure,
Sprinkled all o'er with reconciling blood,
Will I abide, and never wander more,
Walking along in fellowship with God.

H. BONAR.

43. *Isaiah* lxiv. 22. S.M.

1 My sins are blotted out,
Since Jesus died for me;
My times are in a Father's hand,
My steps in His decree.

2 Jesus in heaven appears,
For me to intercede;
And countless benefits proclaim,
"The Lord is risen indeed."

3 A little child is free
Of carefulness and guile,
Rests in a mother's guardian love,
And waits a father's smile.

4 Father of spirits, hear,
Make me this little child;
May I delight myself in Thee,
By no mistrust defiled.

44. *Rev.* xxii. 17–20. S.M.

1 The Spirit in our hearts
Is whispering, Sinner, come!
The bride, the Church of Christ proclaim
To all His children, come.

2 Let him that heareth, say
To all about him, Come!
Let him that thirsts for righteousness,
To Christ, the fountain, come!

3 Yes! whosoever will,
Oh! let him freely come,
And freely drink the stream of life;
'Tis Jesus bids him Come;

4 Lo! Jesus, who invites,
Declares, "I quickly come;"
Lord, even so! I wait Thy hour·
Jesus, my Saviour, come!

45. 2 *Peter* i. 19. **C.M**

1 Hope of our hearts, O Lord, appear,
Thou glorious star of day;
Shine forth and chase the dreary night,
With all our tears, away!

2 Strangers on earth, we wait for Thee;
Oh! leave the Father's throne;
Come with a shout of victory, Lord,
And claim us as Thy own.

3 Oh! bid the bright archangel now,
The trump of God prepare,
To call Thy saints—the quick, the dead,
To meet Thee in the air.

4 No resting-place we seek on earth,
No loveliness we see;
Our eye is on the royal crown
Prepared for us and Thee.

5 But, dearest Lord, however bright
That crown of joy above,
What is it to the brighter hope
Of dwelling in Thy love?

6 What to the joy, the deeper joy,
Unmingled, pure, and free,
Of union with our living Head,
Of fellowship with Thee?

7 This joy e'en now on earth is ours·
But only Lord, above,
Our heart without a pang shall know
The fulness of Thy love.

8 There, near Thy heart, upon the throne,
Thy ransomed bride shall see
What grace was in the bleeding Lamb
Who died to make her free.

46. *Acts* ii. 2. C.M.

1 Spirit Divine! attend our prayer,
And make this house Thy home;
Descend with all Thy gracious power
Oh! come, Great Spirit, come!

2 Come as the light; to us reveal
Our emptiness and woe;
And lead us in those paths of life
Where all the righteous go.

3 Come as the fire, and purge our hearts
Like sacrificial flame;
Let our whole souls an offering be
To our Redeemer's name.

4 Come as the dew, and sweetly bless
This consecrated hour;
May barren minds be taught to own
Thy fertilizing power.

5 Come as the dove, and spread Thy wings,
The wings of peaceful love;
And let the Church on earth become
Blest as the Church above.

47. 1 *Cor.* iii. 22. C.M.

1 If God is mine, then present things
And things to come are mine;
Yea, Christ, His Word, and Spirit too,
And glory all divine.

2 If He is mine, then from His love
He every trouble sends;
All things are working for my good,
And bliss His rod attends.

3 If He is mine, I need not fear
The rage of earth and hell;
He will support my feeble power,
Their utmost force repel.

4 If He is mine, let friends forsake,
Let wealth and honor flee;
Sure He who giveth me Himself
Is more than these to me.

5 If He is mine, I'll boldly pass
Through death's tremendous vale;
He is a solid comfort when
All other comforts fail.

6 Oh! tell me, Lord, that Thou art mine;
What can I wish beside?
My soul shall at the fountain live,
When all the streams are dried.

48. *Rev.* v. 9. C.M.

1 Sing we the song of those who stand
Around the eternal throne,
Of every kindred, clime, and land,
A multitude unknown.

2 Life's poor distinctions vanish here;
To-day, the young, the old,
Our Saviour and His flock appear,
One Shepherd and one fold.

3 Toil, trial, suffering still await
On earth the pilgrim throng;
Yet learn we in our low estate,
The Church triumphant's song.

4 Worthy the Lamb for sinners slain,
Cry the redeemed above,
Blessing and honor to obtain,
And everlasting love.

5 Worthy the Lamb, on earth we sing,
Who died our souls to save.
Henceforth, O Death! where is thy sting?
Thy victory, O Grave?

6 Then hallelujah! power and praise
To God in Christ be given;
May all who now this anthem raise,
Renew the strain in heaven.

MONTGOMERY.

49. *Rev.* xiv. 4. C.M.

1 A pilgrim through this lonely world,
The blessed Saviour passed:
A mourner all His life was He,
A dying Lamb at last.

2 That tender heart that felt for all,
For all its life-blood gave;
It found on earth no resting-place,
Save only in the grave.

3 Such was our Lord; and shall we fear
The cross, with all its scorn?
Or love a faithless, evil world,
That wreathed His brow with thorn?

4 No, facing all its frowns or smiles,
Like Him, obedient still,
We homeward press through storm or
To Zion's blessed hill. [calm,

50. *Luke* xxii. 42. C.M

1 One prayer I have, all prayers in one,
When I am wholly Thine,
Thy will, my God, Thy will be done,
And let that will be mine.

2 All-wise, Almighty, and All-good,
In Thee I firmly trust;
Thy ways, unknown or understood,
Are merciful and just.

3 May I remember, that to Thee,
Whate'er I have I owe;
And back in gratitude from me,
May all Thy bounties flow.

4 Thy gifts are only then enjoyed,
When used as talents lent;
Those talents only well employed
When in Thy service spent.

5 And though Thy wisdom takes away,
Shall I arraign Thy will?
No, let me bless Thy name, and say,
"The Lord is gracious still."

6 A pilgrim through the earth I roam,
Of nothing long possessed;
And all must fail when I go home,
For this is not my rest.

7 Write but my name upon the roll
Of Thy redeemed above;
Then, heart and mind and strength and
I'll love Thee for Thy love. [soul,

51. 1 *Peter* ii. 25. S.M.

1 I was a wandering sheep,
I did not love the fold;
I did not love my Shepherd's voice,
I would not be controlled.

2 I was a wayward child,
I did not love my home;
I did not love my Father's voice,
I loved afar to roam.

3 The Shepherd sought His sheep,
The Father sought His child;
They followed me o'er vale and hill,
O'er desert, waste, and wild.

4 They found me nigh to death,
Famished, and faint, and lone;
They bound me with the bands of love,
They saved the wandering one.

5 They washed my filth away,
They made me clean and fair;
They brought me to my home in peace,
The long-sought wanderer!

6 Jesus my Shepherd is,
'Twas He that loved my soul,
'Twas He that washed me in His blood,
'Twas He that made me whole.

7 'Twas He that sought the lost,
That found the wandering sheep;
'Twas He that brought me to the fold,
'Tis He that still doth keep.

8 I was a wandering sheep,
I would not be controlled;
But now I love the Shepherd's voice,
I love, I love the fold!

9 I was a wayward child,
I once preferred to roam;
But now I love my Father's voice,
I love, I love His home!

H. BONAR.

52. *Rom.* viii. 12. 7, 7, 4.

1 When I listen to Thy word,
In Thy temple cold and dead;
When I cannot see Thee, Lord,
All faith's little day-light fled,
Sun of glory,
Beam again around my head.

2 When Thy statutes I forsake,
When my graces dimly shine,
When Thy covenant I break,
Jesus, then remember Thine;
Check my wanderings,
By a look of love divine.

3 When Thy heavenly dew distils,
And my views, O Lord, are clear,
Clear and bright from Zion's hills,
Temper joys with holy fear;
Keep me watchful,
Safe alone when Thou art near.

4 When afflictions cloud my sky,
When the tide of sorrow flows,
When Thy rod is lifted high,
Let me on Thy love repose;
Stay the rough wind,
When Thy chilling east wind blows.

5 When the vale of death appears,
Faint and cold this mortal clay,
Kind Forerunner, soothe my fears,
Light me through the darksome way;
Break the shadows,
Usher in eternal day.

J. TAYLOR.

53. *Psalm* cxxi. 1. C.M.

1 Welcome days of solemn meeting!
Welcome days of praise and prayer!
Far from earthly scenes retreating,
In your blessings we would share,—
Sacred seasons,
In your blessings we would share.

2 Be Thou near us, blessed Saviour,
Still at morn and eve the same;
Give us faith that cannot waver;
Kindle in us heaven's own flame,—
Blessed Saviour,
Kindle in us heaven's own flame.

3 When the fervent prayer is glowing,
Holy Spirit hear that prayer;
When the song of praise is flowing,
Let that song Thine impress bear,—
Holy Spirit,
Let that song Thine impress bear.

54. *Rev.* v. 6. C.M

1 Earth has engrossed my love too long,
'Tis time I lift mine eyes
Upwards, dear Father, to Thy throne,
And to my native skies.

2 There the blest man, my Saviour, sits,
The God! how bright He shines!
And scatters infinite delights
On countless happy minds.

3 Seraphs with elevated strains,
Compass the throne around;
And move and charm the starry plains,
With an immortal sound.

4 Jesus, the Lord, their harps employs;
Jesus, my God, they sing!
Jesus, the life of both our joys,
Sound sweet from ev'ry string.

5 Now let me mount and join their song,
And be an angel too:
My heart, my ear, my hand, my tongue,—
Here's joyful work for you.

6 I would begin the music here,
And so my soul should rise:
Oh! for some heav'nly notes to bear
My praises to the skies!

7 There ye that love my Saviour, sit,
There I would fain have place,
Among your thrones, or at your feet,
So I might see His face.

55. *Psalm* cxlviii. 14. P M.

1 Nearer, my God, to Thee,—
Nearer to Thee!
E'en though it be a cross
That raiseth me;
Still all my song shall be,
Nearer, my God, to Thee,
Nearer to Thee!

2 Though like a wanderer,
The sun gone down,
Darkness comes over me,
My rest a stone,
Yet in my dreams I'd be
Nearer, my God, to Thee,—
Nearer to Thee!

3 There let my way appear
Steps unto heav'n;
All that Thou sendest me
In mercy giv'n;
Angels to beckon me
Nearer, my God, to Thee,—
Nearer to Thee!

4 Then with my waking thoughts
Bright with Thy praise,
Out of my stony griefs
Bethel I'll raise;
So by my woes to be
Nearer, my God, to Thee,—
Nearer to Thee!

5 And when on joyful wing,
Cleaving the sky;
Sun, moon, and stars forgot,
Upward I fly;
Still all my song shall be,
Nearer, my God, to Thee,—
Nearer to Thee!

56. *Psalm* xxiii. 4. C.M.

1 There is an hour when I must part
With all I hold most dear;
And life, with its best hopes, will then
As nothingness appear.

2 There is an hour when I must sink
Beneath the stroke of death;
And yield to Him who gave it first,
My struggling vital breath.

3 There is an hour when I must stand
Before the judgment-seat;
And all my sins, and all my foes,
In awful vision meet.

4 There is an hour when I must look
On one eternity;
And nameless woe, or blissful life,
My endless portion be.

5 O Saviour, then, in all my need
Be near, be near to me:
And let my soul, by steadfast faith,
Find life and heaven in Thee.

57. *Acts* xxi. 13. I M.

1 When the spark of life is waning,
Weep not for me:
When the languid eye is straining,
Weep not for me.

When the feeble pulse is ceasing,
Start not at its swift decreasing,
'Tis the fettered soul's releasing;
Weep not for me.

2 When the pangs of death assail me,
Weep not for me:
Christ is mine,—He cannot fail me,—
Weep not for me.
Yes! though sin and doubt endeavor
From His love my soul to sever,
Jesus is my strength for ever;—
Weep not for me.

58. 2 *Tim.* iv. 6. P.M

1 I'm going to leave all my sadness,
I'm going to change earth for heaven,
There, there all is peace, all is gladness,
There pureness and glory are given.
Friends, weep not in sorrow of spirit,
But joy that my time here is o'er;
I go the good part to inherit,
Where sorrow and sin are no more.

2 The shadows of evening are fleeing,
Morn breaks on the city of light;
This moment day starts into being,
Eternity bursts on my sight.

The first-born redeemed from all trouble,
(The Lamb that was slain in the throng,)
Their ardor in praising redouble;—
Breaks not on the ear the new song?

3 I'm going to tell their glad story,
To share in their transports of praise,
I'm going in garments of glory,
My voice to unite with their lays.
Ye fetters corrupted, then leave me;
Thou body of sin, droop and die;
Pains of earth, cease ye ever to grieve me,
From you 'tis for ever I fly.

59. *John* xxi. 16. C.M.

1 Do not I love Thee? O my Lord,
Behold my heart, and see!
And cast each hated idol down,
That dares to rival Thee.

2 Do not I love Thee from my soul?
Then let me nothing love;
Dead be my heart to every joy,
When Jesus cannot move.

3 Is not Thy name melodious still,
To mine attentive ear?
Does not each pulse with pleasure bound
My Saviour's voice to hear?

4 Thou know'st I love Thee, gracious Lord
But oh! I long to soar
Far from the sphere of mortal joys,
And learn to love Thee more!

DODDRIDGE.

60. *Exod.* xiv. 15. P.M.

1 Press forward and fear not; the billows may roll,
But the power of Jesus their rage can control;
Though waves rise in anger, their tumults shall cease,
One word of His bidding shall hush them to peace.

2 Press forward and fear not; though trial be near,
The Lord is our refuge—whom then shall we fear?

His staff is our comfort, our safe-guard His rod;
Then let us be steadfast and trust in our God.

3 Press forward and fear not; be strong in the Lord,
In the power of His promise, the truth of His word;
Through the sea and the desert our path-way may tend,
But He who hath saved us will save to the end.

4 Press forward and fear not; we'll speed on our way;
Why should we e'er shrink from our path in dismay?
We tread but the road which our Leader has trod;
Then let us press forward, and trust in our God.

61. *Psalm* cvii. 1, 2. L.M.

1 Let sinners saved give thanks and sing
Of mercies past, of joys to come;
The Lord their Saviour is and king,
The cross their hope, and heaven their home.

2 Let sinners saved give thanks and sing—
Sweet is the subject of their song—
Who, made the children of a king,
Expect to sit in heaven ere long.

3 Let sinners saved give thanks and sing—
The Lord has kept in dangers past;
And oh! sweet thought, the Lord will bring
His people safe to heaven at last.

4 Let sinners saved give thanks and sing—
Of Jesus sing through all their days;
In heaven their golden harps they'll string,
And then for ever sing His praise.

62. *Heb.* xi. 16. S.M.

1 I have a home above,
From sin and sorrow free;
A mansion which eternal love
Designed and formed for me.

2 My Father's gracious hand
Has built this sweet abode;
From everlasting it was planned—
My dwelling-place with God.

3 My Saviour's precious blood
Has made my title sure:
He passed through death's dark raging flood
To make my rest secure.

4 The Comforter is come,
The earnest has been given;
He leads me onward to the home
Reserved for me in heaven.

5 Loved ones are gone before,
Whose pilgrim days are done;
I soon shall greet them on that shore
Where partings are unknown.

63. 2 *Kings* iv. **26.** **S.M.**

1 Beloved, "it is well!"
God's ways are always right;
And perfect love is o'er them all,
Though far above our sight.

2 Beloved, "it is well!"
Though deep and sore the smart,
The hand that wounds knows how to bind
And heal the broken heart.

3 Beloved, "it is well!"
Though sorrow clouds our way,
'Twill only make the joy more dear
That ushers in the day.

4 Beloved, "it is well!"
The path that Jesus trod,
Though rough, and strait, and dark it be,
Leads home to heaven and God.

64. 2 *Thess.* i. 7. P.M.

1 I hear a voice at dawn of day,
And to my heart it seems to say,
When sorrow dims hope's brightest ray,
"There's rest in heaven."

2 I hear it at the evening tide,
When fitful shadows round us glide,
Still whispering gently at my side,
"There's rest in heaven."

3 E'en at noon's busy hour I hear
The same sweet words accost my ear,
With power to stay the rising tear—
"There's rest in heaven."

4 Blest words! which tell of naught but joy,
Of endless rest without alloy,
Well may they oft our thoughts employ—
"There's rest in heaven."

5 Spirit of life and love divine,
Subdue my heart and make it thine,
That I may dwell upon as mine,
That "rest in heaven."

65. *Phil.* iv. 6. C.M.

1 Prayer is the breath of God in man,
Returning whence it came;
Love is the sacred fire within,
And prayer the rising flame.

2 It gives the burdened spirit ease,
And soothes the troubled breast;
Yields comfort to the mourning soul,
And to the weary rest.

3 The prayers and praises of the saints,
Like precious odors sweet,
Ascend and spread a rich perfume
Around the mercy-seat.

4 When God inclines the heart to pray,
He hath an ear to hear;
To Him there's music in a groan,
And beauty in a tear.

5 The humble suppliant can not fail
To have his wants supplied,
Since He for sinners intercedes,
Who once for sinners died.

BEDDOME.

66. *Psalm* xviii. 1. 6. 8.

1 Thee will I love, my strength, my tower;
Thee will I love, my joy, my crown;
Thee will I love with all my power,
In all Thy works, and Thee alone:
Thee will I love till sacred fire
Fills my whole soul with pure desire.

2 Ah! why did I so late Thee know,
Thee lovelier than the sons of men?
Ah! why did I no sooner go
To Thee, the only ease in pain?
Ashamed I sigh and inly mourn,
That I so late to Thee did turn.

3 In darkness willingly I strayed;
I heard Thee, yet from Thee I roved;
Far wide my wandering thoughts were spread,
Thy creatures more than Thee I loved;
And now, if more at length I see,
'Tis through Thy light, and comes from Thee.

4 I thank Thee, uncreated Sun,
That Thy bright beams on me have shined,
I thank Thee, who hast overthrown
My foes, and healed my wounded mind;
I thank Thee, whose enlivening voice
Bids my freed heart in Thee rejoice.

5 Uphold me in the upward race,
Nor suffer me again to stray;
Strengthen my feet with steady pace
Still to press forward in Thy way:
Let all my powers, with all their might
In Thy sole glory now unite.

6 Thee will I love, my joy, my crown,
Thee will I love, my Lord, my God,
Thee will I love, beneath Thy frown,
Or smile—Thy sceptre, or Thy rod;
What though my flesh and heart decay,
Thee shall I love in endless day.

WESLEY

67. *Gal.* vi. 1. P.M

1 Look Thou with pity on a brother's fall,
But dwell not with stern anger on his fault;
The grace of God alone holds thee, holds all;
Were that withdrawn, thou too wouldst swerve and halt.

2 Lead back the wanderer to the Saviour's fold;
That were an action worthy of a saint;
But not in malice let the crime be told,
Nor publish to the world the evil taint.

3 The Saviour suffers when His children slide;
Then is His holy name by men blasphemed,
And He afresh is mocked, and crucified,
Even by those His bitter death redeemed.

4 Rebuke the sin, but yet in love rebuke,
Feel as one member in another's pain;
Wean back the soul that His fair path forsook,
And mighty and eternal is the gain.

68. *Psalm* cxix. 105. C.M.

1 Would'st thou be wise and know the
Lord?
Would'st thou believe aright?
Make the blest volume of His word,
Thy rule, thy guide, thy light.

2 Here is the spring where waters flow,
To quench our heat of sin;
Here is the tree where truth doth grow,
To lead our lives therein.

3 Here is the Judge that stints the strife,
When men's devices fail;
Here is the bread that feeds the life
Which death can not assail.

4 The tidings of salvation dear
Come to our ears from hence;
The fortress of our faith is here,
Our shield, and our defense.

5 Read not this book in any case
But with a single eye;
Read not but first desire God's grace
To understand thereby.

6 Pray still in faith with this respect,
  To fructify therein;
That knowledge may bring this effect,
  To mortify thy sin.

7 Then happy thou in all thy life,
  Whatso to thee befalls;
Yea! doubly happy shalt thou be,
  When God by death thee calls.

GRESSOP.

68. *Thess.* iii. 13. P.M.

1 Breast the wave, Christian, when it is strongest;
Watch for day, Christian, when the night's longest;
Onward and onward still be thine endeavor,
The rest that remaineth will be for ever.

2 Fight the fight, Christian; Jesus is o'er thee;
Run the race, Christian; heaven is before thee;
He who hath promised faltereth never;
The love of eternity flows on for ever.

3 Lift the eye, Christian, just as it closeth;
Raise the heart, Christian, ere it reposeth;
These from the love of Christ nothing shall sever;
Mount when thy work is done—praise Him for ever.

70. *Ezekiel* xi. 16. L.M.

1 Jesus our Lord! to Thee we call,
Thou art our life, our hope, our all;
And we have nowhere else to flee,
No sanctuary, Lord, but Thee.

2 Whatever foes or fears betide,
In Thy dear presence let us hide;
And while we rest our souls on Thee,
Do Thou our sanctuary be.

3 Quickly the day of light draws nigh,
Or we may bow our heads and die;
But, oh! what joy this witness gives!
Jesus, our sanctuary, lives.

4 He from the grave our dust will raise,
We in the heavens shall sing His praise;
And when in glory we appear,
He'll be our sanctuary there.

71. *Eccles.* xi. 6. **S.M.**

1 Sow in the morn thy seed,
At eve hold not thine hand;
To doubt and fear give thou no heed—
Broad-cast it o'er the land.

2 Beside all waters sow,
The high-way furrows stock;
Drop it where thorns and thistles grow,
Scatter it on the rock.

3 The good, the fruitful ground,
Expect not every where;
O'er hill and dale, by plots, 'tis found;
Go forth then every where.

4 Thou know'st not which may thrive,
The late or early sown;
Grace keeps the precious germ alive,
When and wherever strown;

5 And duly shall appear,
In verdure, beauty, strength,
The tender blade, the stalk, the ear,
And the full corn at length.

6 Thou canst not toil in vain;
Cold, heat, and moist, and dry,
Shall foster and mature the grain,
For garners in the sky.

7 Hence, when the glorious end,
The day of God is come,
The angel reapers shall descend,
And heaven cry, "Harvest home."

MONTGOMERY.

72. 1 *Sam.* xi. 12. S.M.

1 And are we yet alive,
And see each other's face?
Glory and praise to Jesus give
For His redeeming grace!

2 Preserved by power divine,
To full salvation here,
Again in Jesu's praise we join,
And in His sight appear.

3 What troubles have we seen,
What conflicts have we passed,
Fightings without and fears within,
Since we assembled last!

4 But out of all the Lord
Hath brought us by His love;
And still He doth his help afford,
And hides our life above.

5 Then let us make our boast
Of His redeeming power,
Which saves us to the uttermost,
Till we can sin no more.

6 Let us take up the cross,
Till we the crown obtain;
And gladly reckon all things loss,
So we may Jesus gain.

WESLEY.

76. *Luke* xviii. 1. L.M.

1 Prayer was appointed to convey
The blessings God designs to give;
Long as they live should Christians pray,
For only while they pray they live.

2 The Christian's heart his prayer indites,
He speaks as prompted from within;
The Spirit his petition writes,
And Christ receives and gives it in

3 And wilt thou in dead silence lie,
When Christ stands waiting for thy
prayer?
My soul, thou hast a Friend on high;
Arise and try thy interest there.

4 If pains afflict or wrongs oppress,
If cares distract or fears dismay,
If guilt deject, if sin distress,
The remedy's before thee—Pray.

5 'Tis prayer supports the soul that's weak,
Though thoughts be broken, language
lame;
Pray if thou canst or canst not speak;
But pray with faith in Jesu's name.

6 Depend on Him—thou canst not fail;
Make all thy wants and wishes known;
Fear not—His merits must prevail;
Ask what thou wilt, it shall be done.

HART.

74. *Romans* xiii. 25. P.M.

1 Soon and for ever the breaking of day
Shall chase all the night-clouds of sor-
row away;
Soon and for ever we'll see as we're seen,
And know the deep meaning of things
that have been—

Where fightings without and conflicts within
Shall weary no more in the warfare with sin—
Where tears and where fears and where death shall be never,
Christians with Christ shall be soon and for ever.

2 Soon and for ever the work shall be done,
The warfare accomplished, the victory won;
Soon and for ever the soldier lay down
The sword for a harp, the cross for a crown:
Then sink not in sorrow, despond not in fear,
A glorious to-morrow is brightening and near,
When—blessed reward for each faithful endeavor—
Christians with Christ shall be, soon and for ever!

75. *Psalm* lxxiii. 25. **P.M.**

1 Pass away earthly joy—
Jesus is mine!
Break every mortal tie—
Jesus is mine!

Dark is the wilderness;
Distant the resting-place;
Jesus alone can bless:
    Jesus is mine!

2 Tempt not my soul away—
    Jesus is mine!
Here would I ever stay—
    Jesus is mine!
Perishing things of clay,
Born but for one brief day,
Pass from my heart away—
    Jesus is mine!

3 Fare ye well, dreams of night—
    Jesus is mine!
Mine is a dawning bright—
    Jesus is mine!
All that my soul has tried
Left but a dismal void;
Jesus has satisfied—
    Jesus is mine!

4 Farewell mortality—
    Jesus is mine!
Welcome eternity—
    Jesus is mine!
Welcome ye scenes of rest,
Welcome ye mansions blest,
Welcome a Saviour's breast—
    Jesus is mine!

76. *Psalm* lxv. 2. C.M.

1 There is an eye that never sleeps
Beneath the wing of night;
There is an ear that never shuts,
When sink the beams of light.

2 There is an arm that never tires,
When human strength gives way;
There is a love that never fails,
When earthly loves decay.

3 That eye is fixed on seraph throngs;
That arm upholds the sky;
That ear is filled with angel songs;
That love is throned on high.

4 But there's a power which man can wield,
When mortal aid is vain,
That eye, that arm, that love to reach,
That listening ear to gain.

5 That power is prayer; which soars on high
Through Jesus to the throne,
And moves the hand which moves the world,
To bring salvation down.

77. *Ezek.* xxxiv. 23. **7.6.**

1 O gracious Shepherd! bind us
With cords of love to Thee,
And evermore remind us
How mercy set us free.
Oh! may Thy Holy Spirit
Set this before our eyes,
That we Thy death and merit
Above all else may prize.

2 We are of our salvation
Assured through Thy love;
Yet oh! on each occasion
How faithless do we prove!
Thou hast our sins forgiven—
Then leaving all behind,
We would press on to heaven,
Bearing the prize in mind.

3 Grant us henceforth, dear Saviour,
While in this vale of tears,
To look to Thee, and never
Give way to anxious fears.
Thou, Lord, wilt not forsake us,
Though we are oft to blame;
Oh! let Thy love then make us
Hold fast Thy faith and name.

78. 1 *John* i. 7. C.M.

1 Walk in the light! so shalt thou know
That fellowship of love,
His Spirit only can bestow,
Who reigns in light above.

2 Walk in the light! and thou shalt find
Thy heart made truly His,
Who dwells in cloudless light enshrined,
In whom no darkness is.

3 Walk in the light! and sin abhorred
Shall ne'er defile again;
The blood of Jesus Christ the Lord
Shall cleanse from every sin.

4 Walk in the light! and e'en the tomb
No fearful shade shall wear;
Glory shall chase away its gloom,
For Christ hath conquered there.

5 Walk in the light! and thou shalt see
Thy path, though thorny, bright,
For God by grace shall dwell in thee,
And God Himself is light.

79. 1 *Peter* ii. 21, 22, 23. C.M.

1 What grace, O Lord, and beauty shone
 Around Thy steps below!
 What patient love was seen in all
 Thy life and death of woe!

2 For ever on Thy burdened heart
 A weight of sorrow hung;
 Yet no ungentle murmuring word
 Escaped Thy silent tongue.

3 Thy foes might hate, despise, revile—
 Thy friends unfaithful prove;
 Unwearied in forgiveness still,
 Thy heart could only love.

4 Oh! give us hearts to love like Thee—
 Like Thee, O Lord, to grieve
 Far more for other's sins, than all
 The wrongs that we receive.

5 One with Thyself, may every eye
 In us, Thy brethren, see
 That gentleness and grace that spring
 From union, Lord, with Thee.

80. *John* xx. 28. **P.M.**

1 Jesus, Thy name I love,
All other names above,
Jesus my Lord!
Oh! Thou art all to me,
Nothing to please I see,
Nothing apart from Thee,
Jesus my Lord!

2 Thou, blessed Son of God,
Hast bought me with Thy blood,
Jesus my Lord!
Oh! how great is Thy love,
All other loves above,
Love that I daily prove,
Jesus my Lord!

3 When unto Thee I flee,
Thou wilt my refuge be,
Jesus my Lord!
What need I now to fear?
What earthly grief or care,
Since Thou art ever near?
Jesus my Lord!

4 Soon Thou wilt come again!
I shall be happy then,
Jesus my Lord!
Then Thine own face I'll see,
Then I shall like Thee be,
Then evermore with Thee,
Jesus my Lord!

81. *Rev.* ii. 28. P.M.

1 There is a morning star, my soul,
There is a morning star;
'Twill soon be near and bright, though now
It seems so dim and far.
And when time's stars have come and gone,
And every mist of earth has flown,
That better star shall rise,
On this world's clouded skies,
To shine for ever.

2 The night is well nigh spent, my soul,
The night is well nigh spent,
And soon above our heads shall shine
A glorious firmament;
Unutterably pure and bright—
The Lamb once slain, its perfect light—
A light unchanging and divine,
A star that shall unclouded shine,
Descending never.

82. 1 *John* iv. 8. P.M

1 We can not always trace the way,
Where Thou, our gracious Lord, dost move,
But we can always surely say,
That Thou art love.

2 When fear its gloomy cloud will fling
O'er earth—our souls to heaven above
As to their sanctuary spring,
For Thou art love.

3 When mystery shrouds our darkened path,
We'll check our dread, our doubts reprove;
In this our soul sweet comfort hath,
That Thou art love.

4 Yes! Thou art love—a truth like this
Can every gloomy thought remove,
And turn all tears, all woes to bliss;
Our God is love.

83. *Psalm* civ. 34. P.M.

1 I journey through a desert drear and wild,
Yet is my heart by such sweet thoughts beguiled,
Of Him on whom I lean, my strength, my stay,
I can forget the sorrows of the way.

2 Thoughts of His *love*—the root of every grace
Which finds in this poor heart a dwelling-place;
The sunshine of my soul, than day more bright,
And my calm pillow of repose by night.

3 Thoughts of His *sojourn* in this vale of tears—
The tale of love unfolded in those years
Of sinless suffering and patient grace,
I love again—and yet again to trace.

4 Thoughts of His *death*—upon the cross I gaze,
And there behold its sad yet healing rays;

Beacon of hope, which lifted up on high,
Illumes with heavenly light the tear-dimmed eye.

5 Thoughts of His *coming*—for that joyful day
In patient hope I watch, and wait, and pray;
The day draws nigh, the midnight shadows flee;
Oh! what a sun-rise will that advent be!

6 Thus, while I journey on my Lord to meet,
My thoughts and meditations are so sweet
Of Him on whom I lean, my strength, my stay,
I can forget the sorrows of the way.

84. *Exodus* xv. 2. 6, 6, 8.

1 Jehovah is our strength,
And He shall be our song;
We shall o'ercome at length,
Although our foes be strong:
In vain doth Satan then oppose,
The Lord is stronger than His foes.

2 The Lord our refuge is,
  And ever will remain;
Since He hath made us His,
  He will our cause maintain:
In vain our enemies oppose,
For God is stronger than His foes.

3 The Lord our portion is,
  What can we wish for more?
As long as we are His,
  We never can be poor:
In vain do earth and hell oppose,
For God is stronger than His foes.

4 The Lord our Shepherd is,
  He knows our every need;
And since we now are His,
  His care our souls will feed:
In vain do sin and death oppose,
For God is stronger than His foes,

5 Our God our Father is,
  Our names are on His heart;
We ever shall be His,
  He ne'er from us will part:
In vain the world and flesh oppose,
For God is stronger than His foes.

35. *John* xvii. 12. **7, 6**

1 O Lamb of God! still keep me
Near to Thy wounded side;
'Tis only then in safety
And peace I can abide!
What foes and snares surround me!
What doubts and fears within!
The grace that sought and found me,
Alone can keep me clean.

2 'Tis only in Thee hiding,
I feel my life secure—
Only in Thee abiding,
The conflict can endure:
Thine arm the vict'ry gaineth
O'er every hateful foe;
Thy love my heart sustaineth
In all its cares and woe.

3 Soon shall my eyes behold Thee
With rapture, face to face;
One half hath not been told me
Of all Thy power and grace:
Thy beauty, Lord, and glory,
The wonders of Thy love,
Shall be the endless story
Of all Thy saints above.

86. *Cant.* ii. 16. **P.M.**

1 Long did I toil, and know no earthly rest;
Far did I rove, and found no certain home;
At last I sought them in His sheltering breast,
Who opes His arms and bids the weary come;
In Christ I found a home, a rest divine,
And I since then am His, and He is mine.

2 Yes! He is mine! and naught of earthly things—
Not all the charms of pleasure, wealth, or power,
The fame of heroes or the pomp of kings—
Could tempt me to forego His love an hour;
"Go, worthless world," I cry, "with all that's thine;
Go, I my Saviour's am, and He is mine."

3 The good I have is from His stores supplied,
The ill is only what He deems the best;

He for my friend, I'm rich with naught
beside,
And poor without Him, though of all
possest:
Changes may come—I take, or I resign,
Content while I am His, and He is mine.

4 Whate'er may change, in Him no change
is seen—
A glorious sun that wanes not, nor
declines;
Above the clouds and storms He walks
unseen,
And sweetly on His people's darkness
shines:
All may depart—I fret not nor repine,
While I my Saviour's am, and He is mine.

5 While here alas! I know but half His
love,
But half discern Him, and but half
adore;
But when I meet Him in the realms
above,
I hope to love Him better, praise Him
more,
And feel and tell amid the choir divine,
How fully I am His, and He is mine.

87. *Psalm* lvii. 1. C.M.

1 Be merciful to me, O God!
Be merciful to me,
For though I sink beneath Thy rod,
Yet do I trust in Thee.

2 Thou art my refuge, and I know
My burden Thou dost bear,
And I would seek, where'er I go,
To cast on Thee my care.

3 Thou knowest, Lord, my flesh how frail,
Strong though my spirit be;
Oh! then assist, when foes assail,
The soul that clings to Thee.

4 And, gracious Lord, whate'er befall,
A thankful heart be mine—
A heart that answers to Thy call,
One that is wholly Thine.

5 And may I ne'er forget that Thou
Wilt soon return again,
And those who love Thy coming now
Shall shine in glory then.

88. *Psalm* cxlix. 1–4. **P.M.**

1 Praise ye Jehovah, praise the Lord most holy,
Who cheers the contrite, girds with strength the weak;
Praise Him who will with glory crown the lowly,
And with salvation beautify the meek.

2 Praise ye the Lord for all His loving-kindness,
And all the tender mercies He hath shown;
Praise Him who pardons all our sin and blindness,
And calls us sons, and takes us for His own.

3 Praise ye Jehovah! source of every blessing—
Before His gifts earth's richest boons are dim;
Resting in Him, His peace and joy possessing,
All things are ours, for we have all in Him.

4 Praise ye the Father! God the Lord who gave us,
With full and perfect love, His only Son;
Praise ye the Son who died Himself to save us!
Praise ye the Spirit! praise the Three in One.

89. *Psalm* xxxii. 7. Double C.M

1 Thou art my hiding-place, O Lord!
In Thee I put my trust;
Encouraged by Thy holy word,
A feeble child of dust:
I have no argument beside,
I urge no other plea;
And 'tis enough my Saviour died,
My Saviour died for me!

2 When storms of fierce temptation beat,
And furious foes assail,
My refuge is the mercy-seat,
My hope within the vail.
From strife of tongues and bitter words,
My spirit flies to Thee;
Joy to my heart the thought affords,
My Saviour died for me!

3 'Mid trials heavy to be borne,
When mortal strength is vain—
A heart with grief and anguish torn—
A body racked with pain—
Ah! what could give the sufferer rest,
Bid every murmur flee,
But this, the witness in my breast,
My Saviour died for me!

4 And when Thine awful voice commands
This body to decay,
And life in its last lingering sands,
Is ebbing fast away—
Then, though it be in accents weak,
And faint and tremblingly,
Oh! give me strength in death to speak,
"My Saviour died for me!"

RAFFLES.

90. *Coloss.* iii. 11. **P.M.**

1 Jesus, my Saviour, look on me!
For I am weary and opprest;
I come to cast my soul on Thee;
Thou art my rest.

2 Look down on me, for I am weak;
I feel the toilsome journey's length;
Thine aid omnipotent I seek;
Thou art my strength.

3 I am bewildered on my way;
Dark and tempestuous is the night;
Oh! shed Thou forth some cheering ray;
Thou art my light.

4 I hear the storms around me rise,
But, when I dread th' impending shock,
My spirit to her refuge flies;
Thou art my rock.

5 When the accuser flings his darts,
I look to Thee—my terrors cease;
Thy cross a hiding-place imparts;
Thou art my peace.

6 Standing alone on Jordan's brink,
In that tremendous, latest strife,
Thou wilt not suffer me to sink;
Thou art my life.

7 Thou wilt my every want supply,
Even to the end, whate'er befall;
Through life, in death, eternally,
Thou art my all.

MACDUFF.

91. *Heb.* iv. 15. **C.M.**

1 Jesus, my sorrow lies too deep
For human ministry:
It knows not how to tell itself
To any but to Thee.

2 Thou dost remember still, amid
The glories of God's throne,
The sorrows of mortality,
For they were once Thine own.

3 Yes! for as if Thou would'st be God,
E'en in Thy misery,
There's been no sorrow but Thine own
Untouched by sympathy.

4 Jesus, my fainting spirit rings
Its fearfulness to Thee;
Thine eye at least can penetrate
The clouded mystery.

5 It is enough, my precious Lord,
Thy tender sympathy!
There is no sorrow e'er so deep
But I may bring to Thee.

92. 1 *Peter* i. 8. 8. 8. 6.

1 Jesus, I love Thee! Thou dost know
How true my love, how deep my woe;
Almost too deep to bear!
But Thou wilt guide me by Thy hand,
Strong in Thy strength I yet may stand,
Still resting in Thy care.

2 Thou wilt not leave the weakest one;
Though every outward hope be gone,
I know that Thou art nigh;
Man knows not what my sufferings are,
He can not know; he would not care;
But Thou art sympathy.

3 Thou wilt not let my footsteps fail,
Nor let me, journeying through this vale,
Bring on Thy Gospel shame;
Though naught is mine but sin and woe,
Yet in Thy righteousness I go,
And triumph in Thy name.

4 And when the bitter cup is past,
And when I sink in death at last,
It is to be with Thee;
To come with Thee in clouds of heaven,
Ransomed, pure, holy, Thine, forgiven,
Ever to reign with Thee.

93. *Psalm* xxxix. 9. **S.M.**

1 It is Thy hand, my God!
My sorrow comes from Thee—
I bow beneath Thy chastening rod;
'Tis love that bruises me.

2 I would not murmur, Lord,
Before Thee I am dumb—
Lest I should breathe one murmuring word,
To Thee for help I come.

My God! Thy name is Love,
A Father's hand is Thine;
With tearful eye I look above,
And cry, "Thy will be mine."

4 I know Thy will is right,
Though it may seem severe;
Thy path is still unsullied light,
Though dark it oft appear.

5 Jesus for me hath died;
Thy Son Thou didst not spare;
His pierced hands, His bleeding side,
Thy love for me declare

6 Here my poor heart can rest—
 My God! it cleaves to Thee;
Thy will is love, Thine end is blest,
 All work for good to me.

94. *Isaiah* xlii. 16. P.M.

1 I know not the way I am going,
 But well do I know my Guide;
With a child-like trust I give my hand
 To the mighty Friend by my side.
The only thing that I say to Him,
 As He takes it, is: "Hold it fast,
Suffer me not to lose my way,
 And bring me home at last."

2 As when some helpless wanderer,
 Alone in an unknown land,
Tells the guide his destined place of rest,
 And leaves all else in his hand:
'Tis home, 'tis home that we wish to reach;
 He who guides us may choose the way;
Little we heed what path we take.
 If nearer home each day.

95. *Rom.* xiii. 11. **P.M.**

1 One sweetly solemn thought,
Comes to me o'er and o'er—
I am nearer home to-day
Than I ever have been before.

2 Nearer my Father's house,
Where the many mansions be;
Nearer the great white throne;
Nearer the crystal sea;

3 Nearer the bound of life,
Where we lay our burdens down;
Nearer leaving the cross;
Nearer gaining the crown.

4 But lying darkly between,
Winding down through the night,
Is the deep and unknown stream,
That leads at last to the light.

5 Jesus, perfect my trust,
Strengthen the hand of my faith;
Let me feel Thee near when I stand
On the edge of the shore of death.

6 Feel Thee near when my feet
Are slipping over the brink;
For it may be, I'm nearer home—
Nearer now than I think.

CAREY.

96. *1 Thess.* iv. 14. L.M.

1 Asleep in Jesus! blessed sleep!
From which none ever wakes to weep;
A calm and undisturbed repose,
Unbroken by the last of foes!

2 Asleep in Jesus! oh! how sweet
To be for such a slumber meet!
With holy confidence to sing,
That death has lost his venomed sting!

3 Asleep in Jesus! peaceful rest!
Whose waking is supremely blest:
No fear, no woe shall dim that hour
That manifests the Saviour's power.

4 Asleep in Jesus! oh! for me
May such a blissful refuge be!
Securely shall my ashes lie,
Waiting the summons from on high.

5 Asleep in Jesus! time nor space
Debars this precious hiding-place;
On Indian plains or Northern snows
Believers find the same repose.

6 Asleep in Jesus! far from Thee
Thy kindred and their graves may be!
But thine is still a blessed sleep,
From which none ever wakes to weep.

97. *Heb.* iv. 3. P.M.

1 Jesus, we rest in Thee,
In Thee ourselves we hide;
Laden with guilt and misery,
Where could we rest beside?
'Tis on Thy meek and lowly breast
Our weary souls alone can rest.

2 Thou holy One of God!
The Father rests in Thee,
And in the savor of that blood
Once shed on Calvary.
The curse is gone—through Thee we're blest;
God rests in Thee—in Thee we rest.

3 The slaves of sin and fear—
    Thy truth our bondage broke;
  Our happy spirits love to wear
    Thy light and easy yoke.
  The love which fills our grateful breast
  Makes duty joy, and labor rest.

4 Soon the bright, glorious day—
    The rest of God shall come;
  Sorrow and sin shall pass away,
    And we shall reach our home:
  Then of the promised land possessed,
  Our souls shall know eternal rest.

98. 1 *Thess.* iv. 13. C.M.

1 Take comfort, Christians, when your friends
    In Jesus fall asleep;
  Their better being never ends—
    Why then dejected weep?

2 Why inconsolable, as those
    To whom no hope is given?
  Death is the messenger of peace,
    And calls the soul to heaven.

3 As Jesus died, and rose again,
Victorious from the dead;
So His disciples rise, and reign
With their triumphant Head.

4 The time draws nigh, when from the clouds
Christ shall with shouts descend;
And the last trumpet's awful voice
The heavens and earth shall rend.

5 Then they who live shall changed be,
And they who sleep shall wake;
The graves shall yield their ancient charge,
And earth's foundations shake.

6 The saints of God, from death set free,
With joy shall mount on high;
The heavenly hosts with praises loud,
Shall meet them in the sky.

Together to their Father's house,
With joyful hearts they go;
And dwell for ever with the Lord,
Beyond the reach of woe.

8 A few short years of evil past,
We reach the happy shore,
Where death-divided friends at last
Shall meet to part no more.

99. *Acts* vii. 59. **P.M.**

1 My soul, go boldly forth,
Forsake this sinful earth;
What hath it been to thee
But pain and sorrow?
And think'st thou it will be
Better to-morrow?

2 Why art thou for delay?
Thou cam'st not here to stay;
What tak'st thou for thy part
But heavenly pleasure?
Where then should be thy heart
But where's thy treasure?

3 Thy God, thy Head's above;
There is the world of love;
Mansions there purchased are,
By Christ's own merit,
For these He doth prepare
Thee by His Spirit.

4 Lord Jesus, take my spirit,
I trust Thy love and merit:
Take home Thy wand'ring sheep,
For Thou hast sought it;
My soul in safety keep,
For Thou hast bought it.

BAXTER.

100. 2 *Tim.* iv. 6. L.M.

1 The hour of my departure's come,
I hear the voice that calls me home
At last, O Lord! let trouble cease,
And let Thy servant die in peace.

2 Not in mine innocence I trust;
I bow before Thee in the dust;
And through my Saviour's blood alon
I look for mercy at Thy throne.

3 I leave the world without a tear,
Save for the friends I held so dear,
To heal their sorrows, Lord, descend,
And to the friendless prove a friend.

4 I come, I come at Thy command,
I give my spirit to Thy hand;
Stretch forth Thine everlasting arms,
And shield me in the last alarms.

5 The hour of my departure's come,
I hear the voice that calls me home;
Now, oh! my God, let trouble cease,
Now let Thy servant die in peace.

LOGAN.

They sung as it were a new song before the throne." (Rev. xiv. 3.)

INDEX TO FIRST LINES.

www.ingramcontent.com/pod-product-compliance
Lightning Source LLC
LaVergne TN
LVHW021423110826
845150LV00007B/2054

* 9 7 8 1 4 2 5 5 0 8 6 6 1 *